Fierce Fighters
GREEK WARRIORS

Charlotte Guillain

Raintree
Chicago, Illinois

www.heinemannraintree.com
Visit our website to find out
more information about
Heinemann-Raintree books.

To order:

☎ Phone 888-454-2279

💻 Visit www.heinemannraintree.com
to browse our catalog and order online.

©2010 Raintree
an imprint of Capstone Global Library, LLC
Chicago, Illinois

Edited by Rebecca Rissman, Nancy Dickmann,
and Catherine Veitch
Designed by Joanna Hinton-Malivoire
Original illustrations © Capstone Global Library 2010
Original illustrations by Miracle Studios
Picture research by Tracy Cummins
Production by Victoria Fitzgerald
Originated by Capstone Global Library
Printed and bound in China by Leo Paper Products Ltd

14 13 12 11 10
10 9 8 7 6 5 4 3 2 1

**Library of Congress Cataloging-in-
Publication Data**

Guillain, Charlotte.
  Greek warriors / Charlotte Guillain.
    p. cm. -- (Fierce fighters)
  Includes bibliographical references and index.
  ISBN 978-1-4109-3766-7 (hard cover) -- ISBN 978-
1-4109-3774-2 (pbk.) 1. Military art and science--
Greece--History--To 500--Juvenile literature. 2. Soldiers-
-Greece--History--Juvenile literature. 3. Weapons,
Ancient--Greece--Juvenile literature. 4. Greece--History,
Military--To 146 B.C.--Juvenile literature. I. Title.
  U33.G85 2010
  938--dc22
                    2009030861

Acknowledgments
We would like to thank the following for permission to
reproduce photographs: Alamy pp. **9** (© Photos 12), **17**
(© Peter Horree), **24** (© North Wind Picture Archives),
25 (© The London Art Archive); Art Resource, NY pp.
13 (Réunion des Musées Nationaux), **18** (Erich Lessing);
Corbis pp. **11** (© René Mattes/Hemis), **26** (© Charles
& Josette Lenars), **7** (©Dallas and John Heaton); Getty
Images pp. **10** (Penelope Painter), **23** (Charles Le Brun);
Heinemann Raintree pp. **28** (Karon Dubke), **29 top**
(Karon Dubke), **29 bottom** (Karon Dubke); Shutterstock
p. **19** (© bkp); The Art Archive pp. **12** (Archaeological
Museum Ferrara / Alfredo Dagli Orti), **14** (Museo di
Villa Giulia Rome / Gianni Dagli Orti), **22** (Staatliche
Glyphothek Munich / Alfredo Dagli Orti); The Granger
Collection, New York p. **27**.

Front cover photograph of a Greek battle reproduced
with permission of Miracle Studios.

The publishers would like to thank Jane Penrose for her
assistance in the preparation of this book.

Some words are shown in bold, **like this.** You can find
out what they mean by looking in the glossary.

Contents

Grim Greeks

Place: Greece
Date: 431 BCE

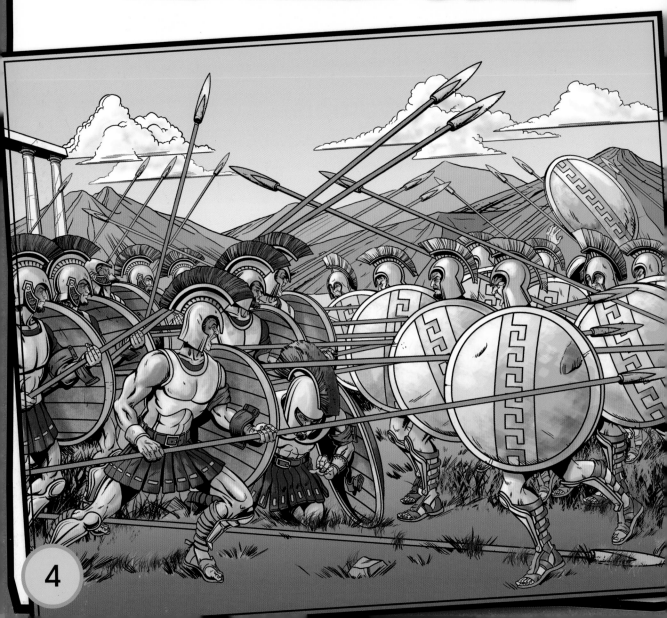

Two armies are marching toward each other. Suddenly the enemies smash into each other. Swords and **spears** clash. **Warriors** roar. Dying soldiers scream.

The Greek armies are at war again!

Greek timeline

776 BCE	First Olympic Games in Greece
460-340 BCE	Many battles between Sparta and other Greek city-states
146 BCE	Rome conquers Greece
1400s CE	Columbus sails to America
1600s	People from Europe start to settle in North America
2000s	You are reading this book

Who Were the Ancient Greeks?

Ancient Greece was made up of different cities and the land around them, called **city-states**. Each city-state had a ruler. These rulers often fought one another to get more land and become more powerful.

The ancient Greek Empire

Key

■ ancient Greek Empire

— country border today

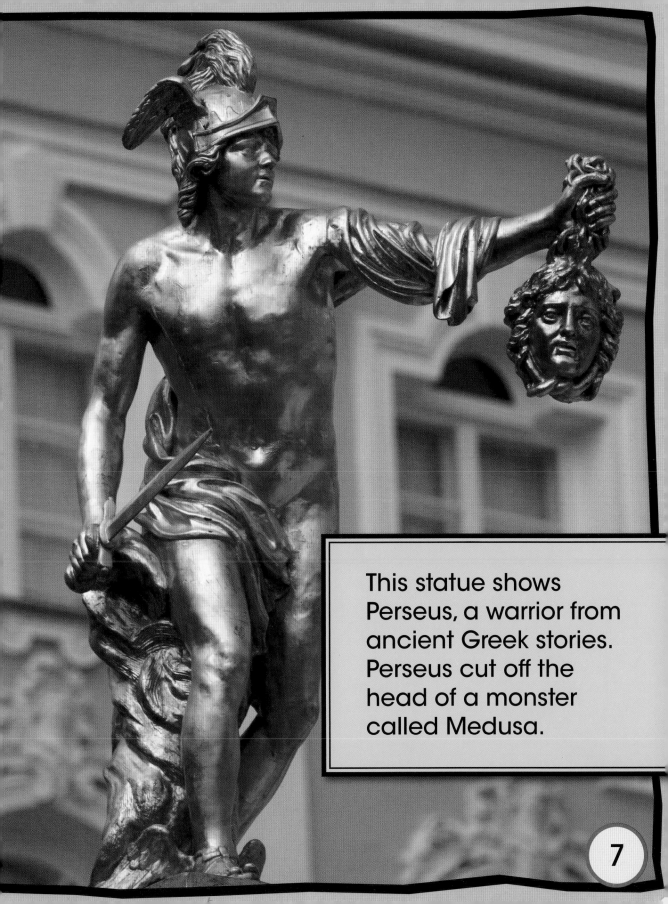

This statue shows Perseus, a warrior from ancient Greek stories. Perseus cut off the head of a monster called Medusa.

Becoming a Greek Warrior

In Athens young Greek men had to train as soldiers for two years. They had to buy their own **armor** and weapons. After two years they finished training and only had to fight if their ruler started a war.

We can learn about ancient Greek heroes from films.

In Sparta all boys started training as soldiers when they were seven years old. They played a lot of sports and practiced using their weapons. Groups of boys had to fight one another so they would become mean and **violent**.

This jar shows two boys learning to fight.

DID YOU KNOW?

Twelve-year-old Spartan boys had to wear the same thin **tunic** all year long to make them tough.

Fighting Wars

When a ruler went to war, all men would fight in the army. They wanted to **protect** their homes and families. Soldiers in the same army painted their shields with the same colors. Then they knew who the enemy was as they fought.

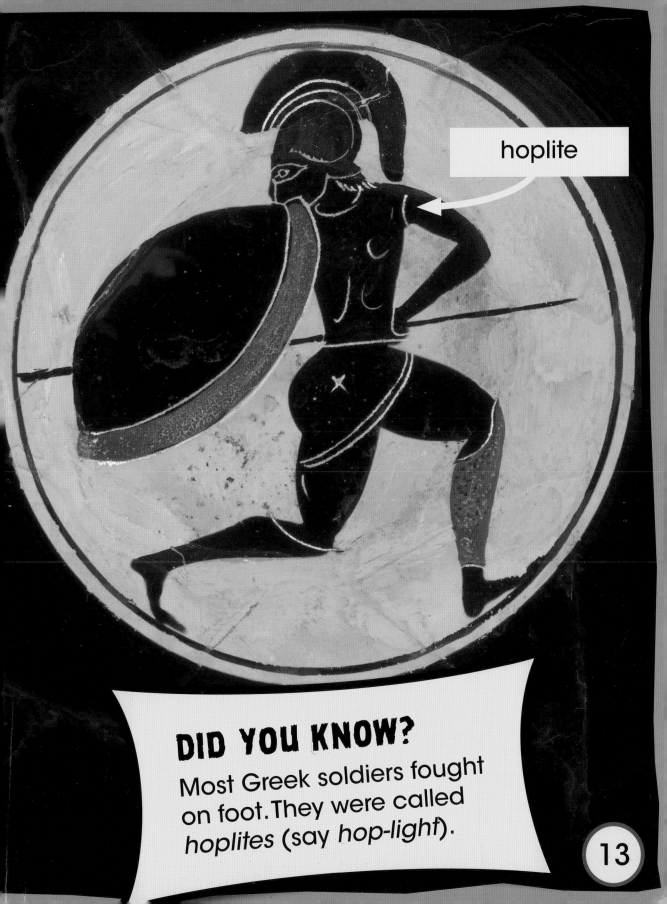

hoplite

DID YOU KNOW?

Most Greek soldiers fought on foot. They were called *hoplites* (say *hop-light*).

13

Foot soldiers had to be very fit and skilled. But they also had to work as a team. They ran at the enemy in a tight rectangle called a **phalanx** (say *fa-lanks*). They held up their shields together and stuck out their **spears**.

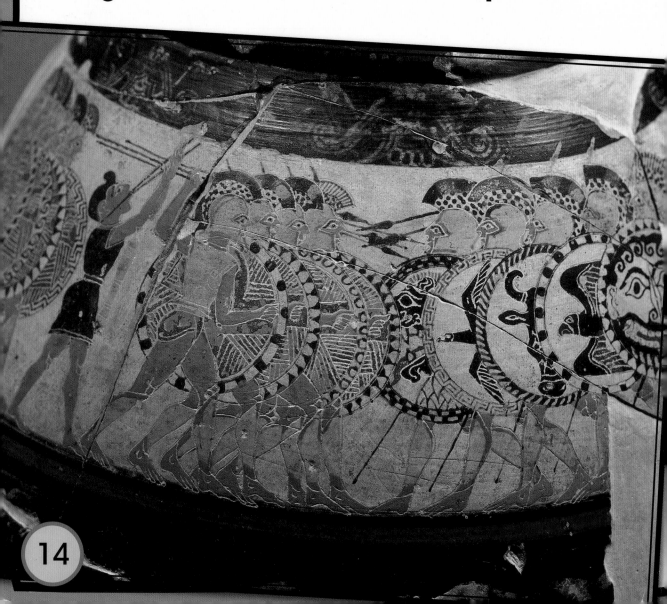

DID YOU KNOW?

When the soldiers in a phalanx held up their shields, the shields overlapped. This made it hard for the enemy to attack.

Some **city-states** had special soldiers who fought on their own. They ran at the enemy, throwing **spears** and breaking up the **phalanxes**.

DID YOU KNOW?

Other soldiers galloped into battle on horses. This was a scary sight for the foot soldiers.

Greek Weapons

Most of the soldiers in a Greek army wore **armor** and metal helmets and carried a wooden shield. Most foot soldiers carried a long spear called a **dory** and a sword. Some Greek warriors also used bows and arrows.

bow and arrow

Other soldiers were stone-slingers. They used a special **sling** to throw stones into battle. The stones could hit their enemies on the head. But sometimes they hit their own army by mistake!

sling

DID YOU KNOW?
Some soldiers trained to throw stones by hand, without a sling.

Famous Greek Warriors

Alexander the Great was a king in the north of Greece. Alexander was a strong leader who knew how to beat his enemies and win a war.

Alexander the Great

DID YOU KNOW?

Alexander built many new cities and often called them "Alexandria" after himself!

Greek Women

Most Greek women had to stay at home and take care of children. But in Sparta things were different. Spartan women ran in races, wrestled, and played sports. They brought up their children to know how to fight.

Spartan girl

DID YOU KNOW?

Ancient Greek stories told of warrior women called the Amazons. They were ruled by a queen and kept men as **slaves**.

Greeks Versus Romans

In the end the Roman army beat the Greek **warriors**. The Romans took over all the Greek lands and became the most powerful rulers in the world. The days of Greek warriors were over.

Roman soldiers

This statue shows a
fallen Greek soldier.

Greek Warrior Activity

Greek soldiers ate sesame seeds to give them energy as they marched into battle.

Make your own sesame buns

You will need:
- 2 cups whole wheat flour
- 1 cup milk
- 3/4 cup olive oil
- 3 eggs
- 1 teaspoon salt
- 3/4 cup sesame seeds
- 1 cup honey

1. Preheat the oven to 350°F (180°C).

2. Mix the salt with the flour and add the olive oil and eggs. **Knead** the mixture.

3. Add the milk, half the honey, and half the sesame seeds.

 **Always have an adult with you when you are cooking.**

4. Form the mixture into bun shapes. Put them on a baking tray.

5. Make a small hole in the middle of each bun. Fill the holes with the rest of the honey. Sprinkle the rest of the sesame seeds over the buns.

6. Bake for 40 minutes, until they are golden brown.

Glossary

armor leather or metal covering to protect a soldier

city-state area made up of a city and the land and villages around it. Each city-state had its own ruler.

dory a long, light spear used as a weapon by Greek warriors

knead press down dough with hands

phalanx group of soldiers moving closely together into battle

protect keep from getting hurt

slave person who is owned by someone else. Slaves had to work hard and did not get paid.

sling strap used to throw a stone as a weapon

spear weapon with sharp blade on a long pole

tunic loose piece of clothing with no sleeves

violent behaving in a rough way that will hurt others

warrior fighter

Find Out More

Books

Charman, Andrew. *Life and Times in Ancient Greece.* New York: Kingfisher, 2007.

Claybourne, Anna. *Time Travel Guide: Ancient Greece.* Chicago: Heinemann-Raintree, 2008.

Pepper, Cary. Ancient Greece. Mankato, Minn.: Capstone Press, 2010.

Websites

www.historyforkids.org/learn/greeks/war/
Learn all about ancient Greek warfare.

www.ancientgreece.co.uk
Learn about the Ancient Greeks on this British Museum website.

http://greece.mrdonn.org/alexander.html
Learn about Alexander the Great and his empire, as well as other facts about ancient Greece.

Find out

Name a race that the ancient Greeks took part in.

Index